WRITE YOUR OWN CREATIVE SHORT STORIES

(With Picture Prompts)

THIS BOOK BELONGS TO:

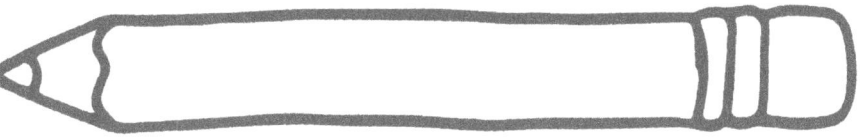

WRITE A SHORT STORY ABOUT WHAT YOU SEE

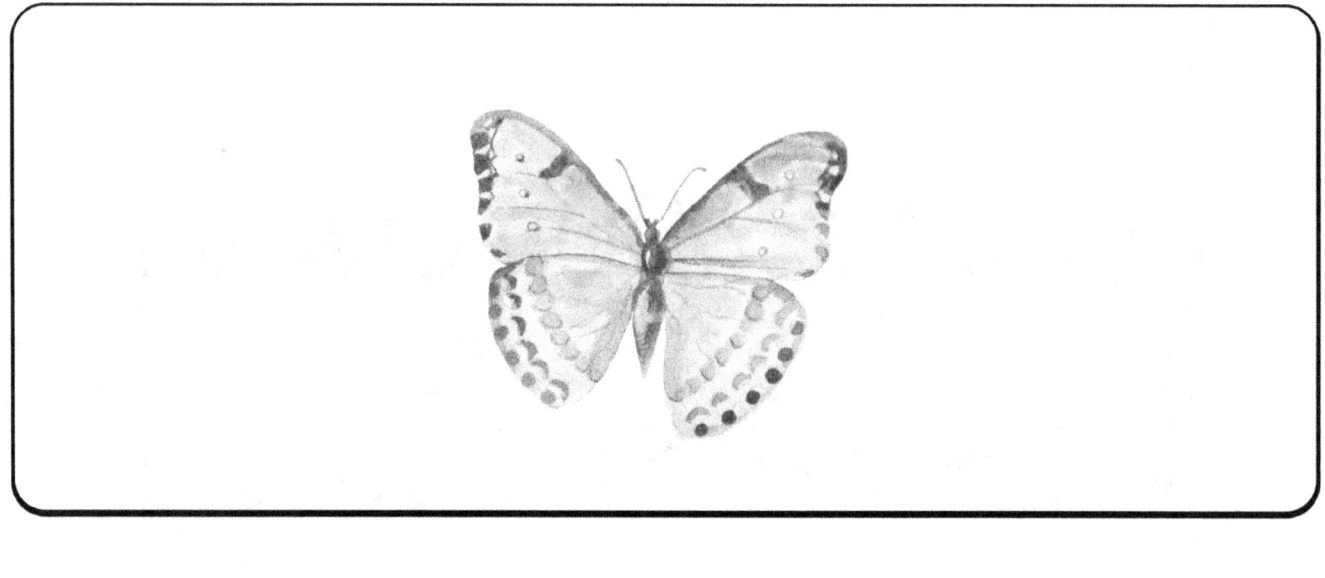

WRITE A SHORT STORY ABOUT WHAT YOU SEE

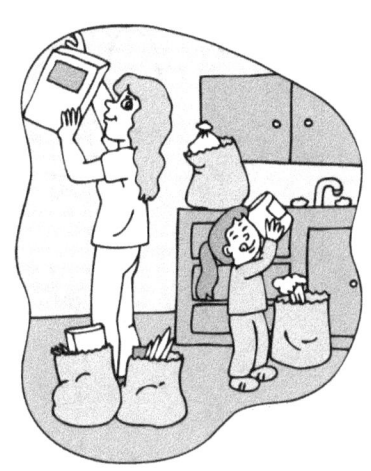

WRITE A SHORT STORY ABOUT WHAT YOU SEE

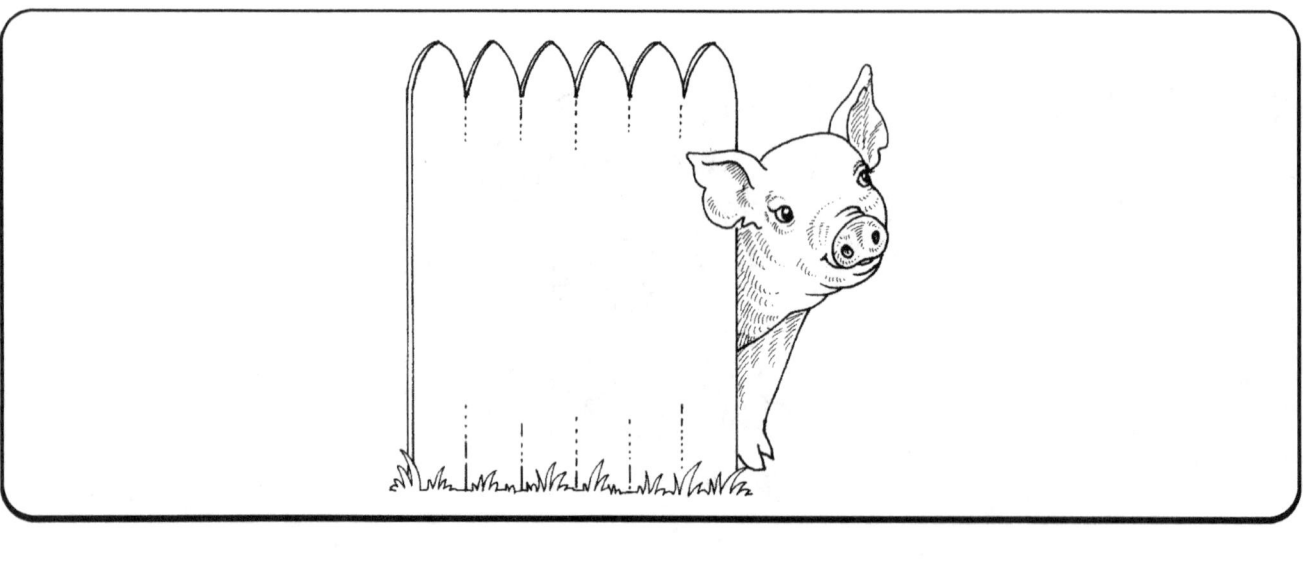

WRITE A SHORT STORY ABOUT WHAT YOU SEE

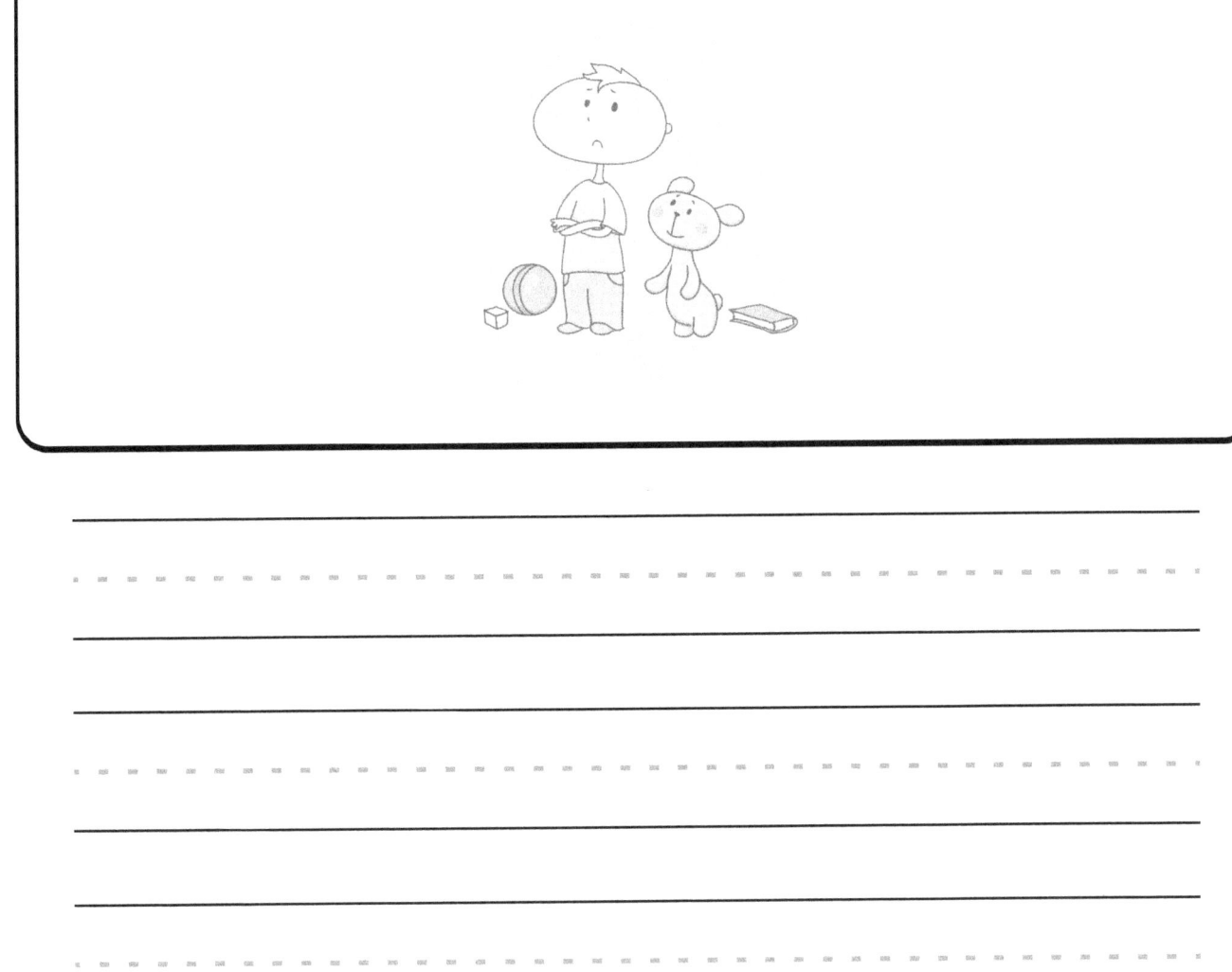

WRITE A SHORT STORY ABOUT WHAT YOU SEE

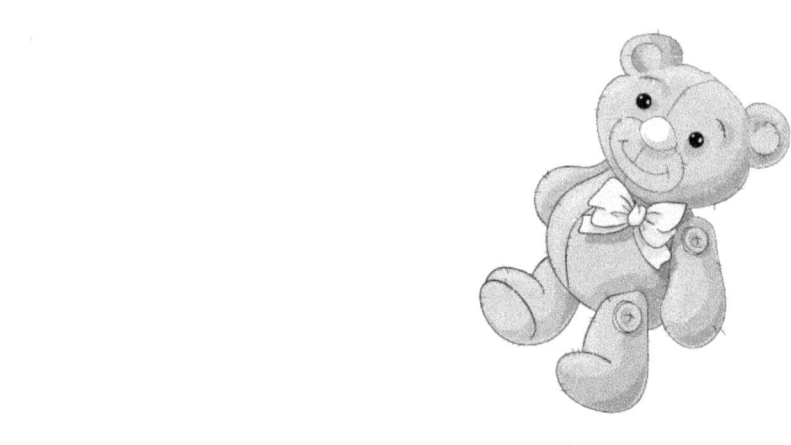

WRITE A SHORT STORY ABOUT WHAT YOU SEE

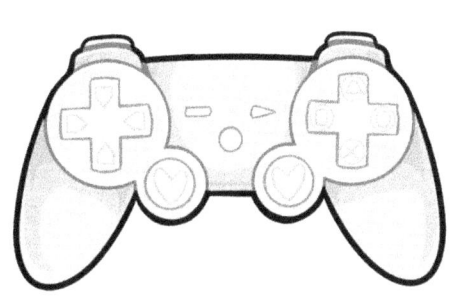

WRITE A SHORT STORY ABOUT WHAT YOU SEE

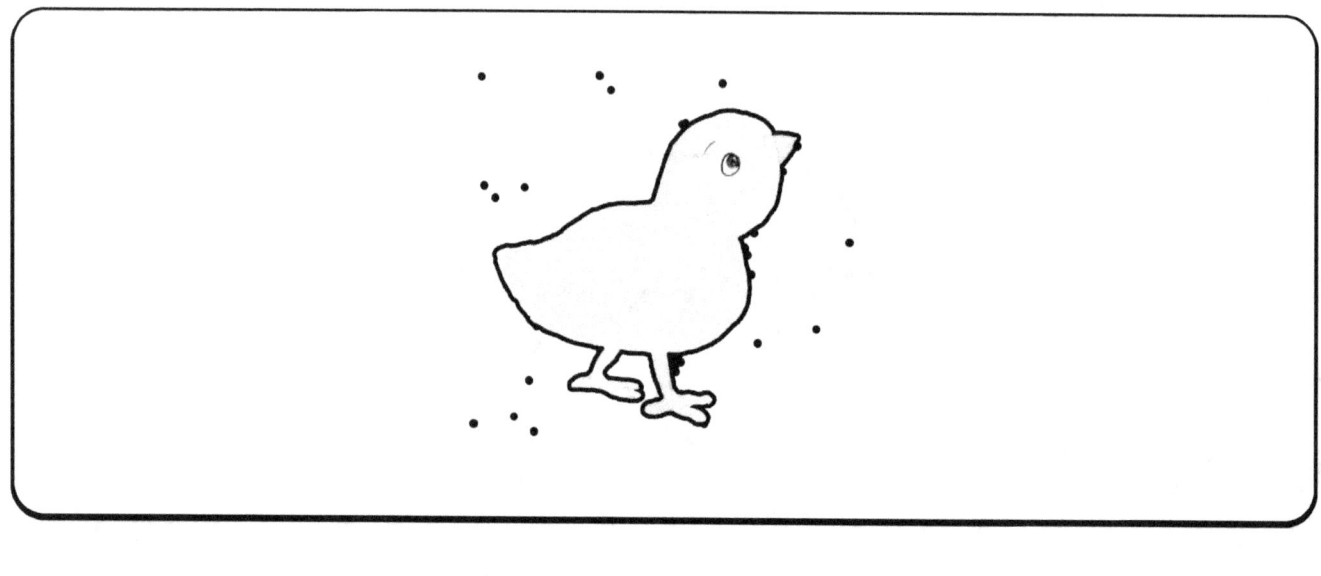

WRITE A SHORT STORY ABOUT WHAT YOU SEE

WRITE A SHORT STORY ABOUT WHAT YOU SEE

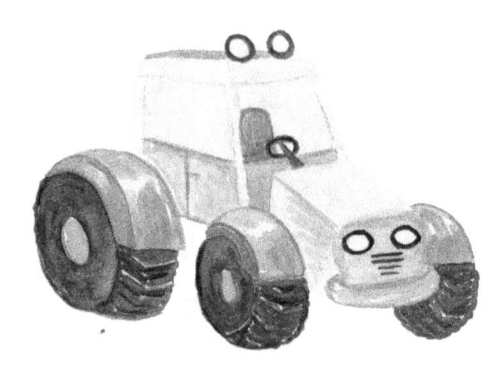

WRITE A SHORT STORY ABOUT WHAT YOU SEE

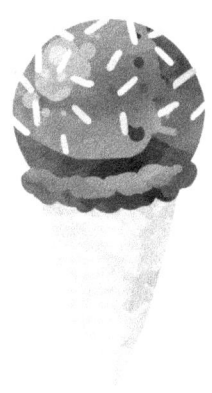

WRITE A SHORT STORY ABOUT WHAT YOU SEE

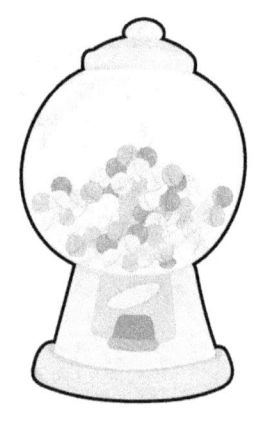

WRITE A SHORT STORY ABOUT WHAT YOU SEE

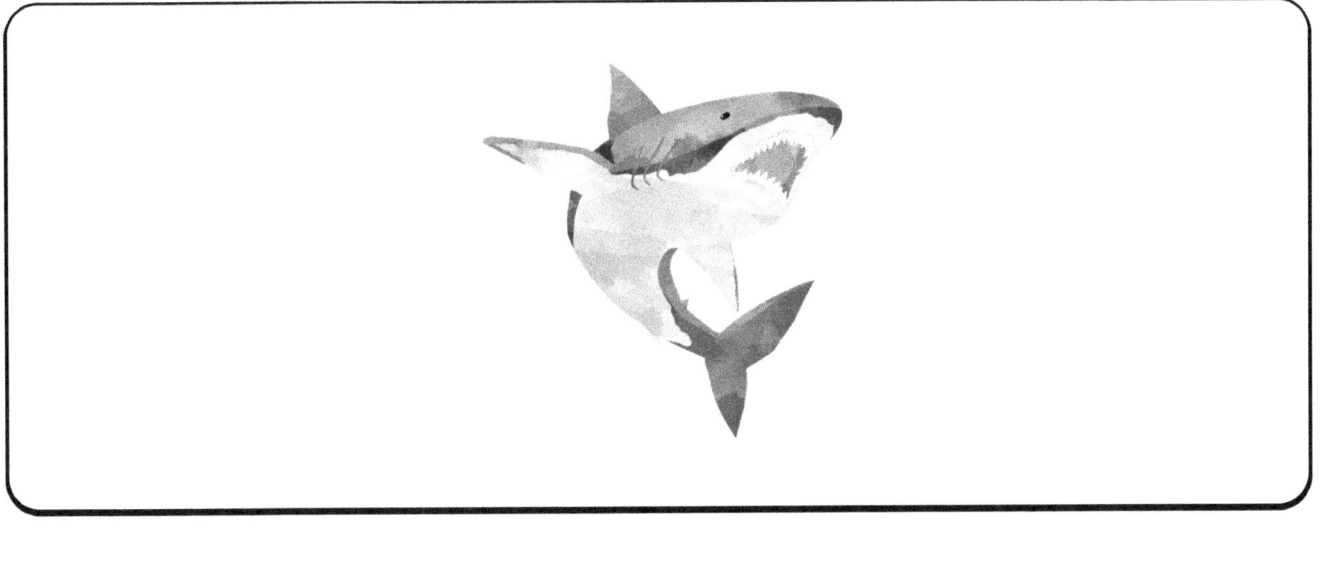

WRITE A SHORT STORY ABOUT WHAT YOU SEE

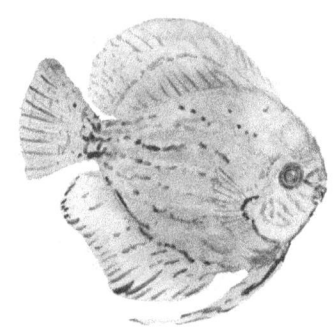

WRITE A SHORT STORY ABOUT WHAT YOU SEE

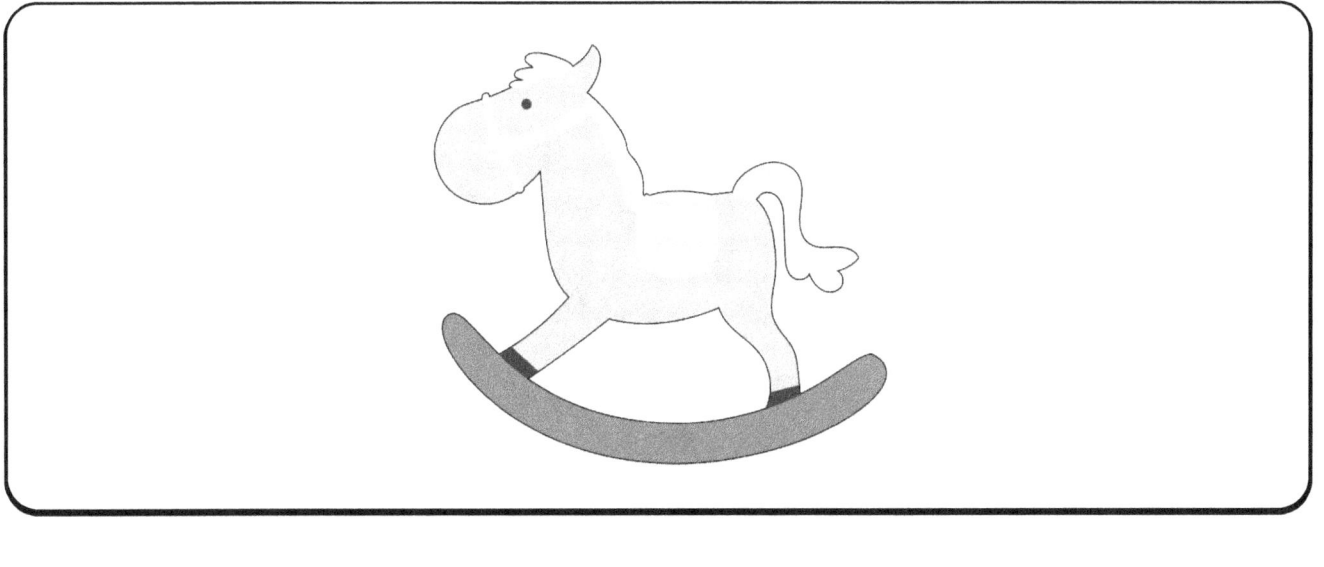

WRITE A SHORT STORY ABOUT WHAT YOU SEE

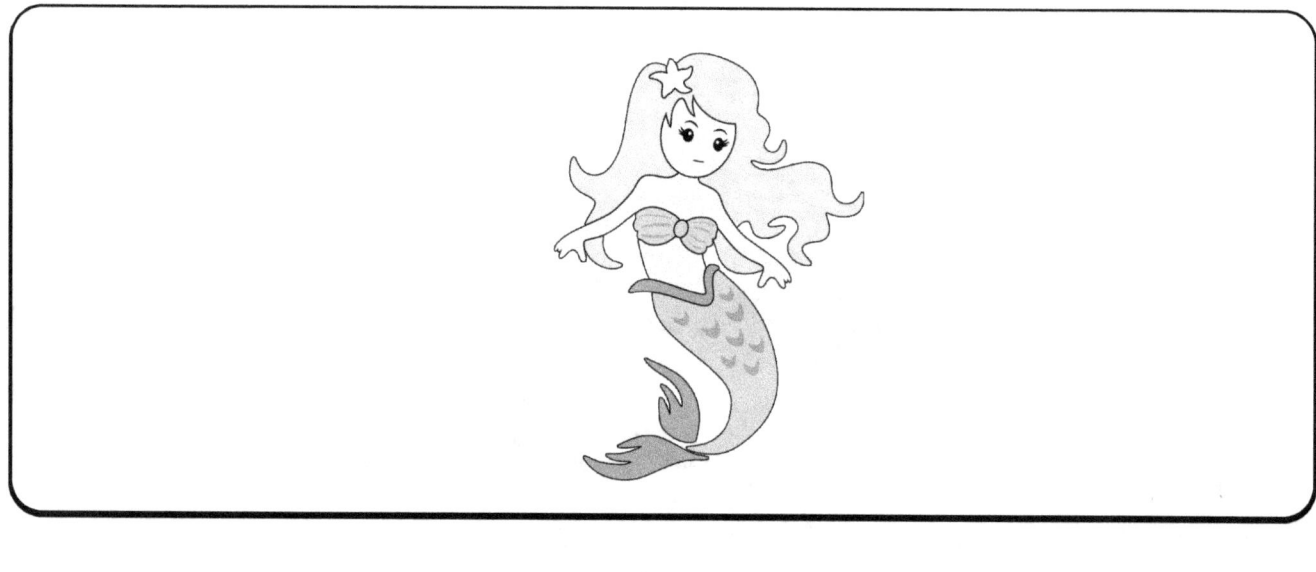

WRITE A SHORT STORY ABOUT WHAT YOU SEE

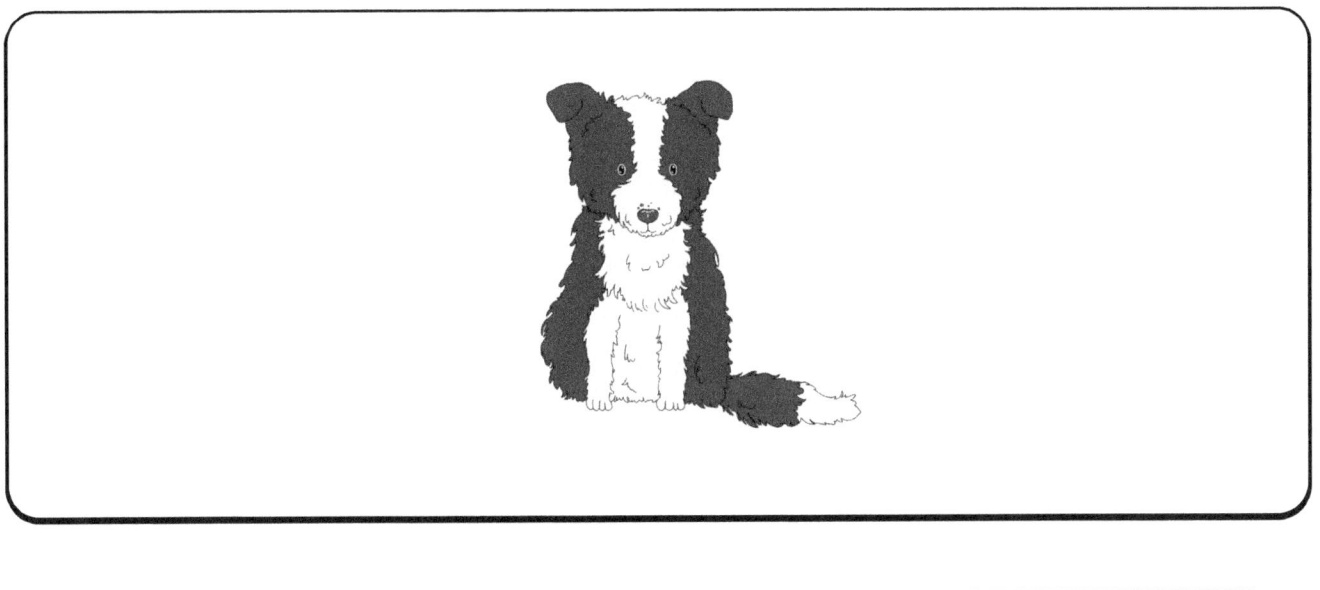

WRITE A SHORT STORY ABOUT WHAT YOU SEE

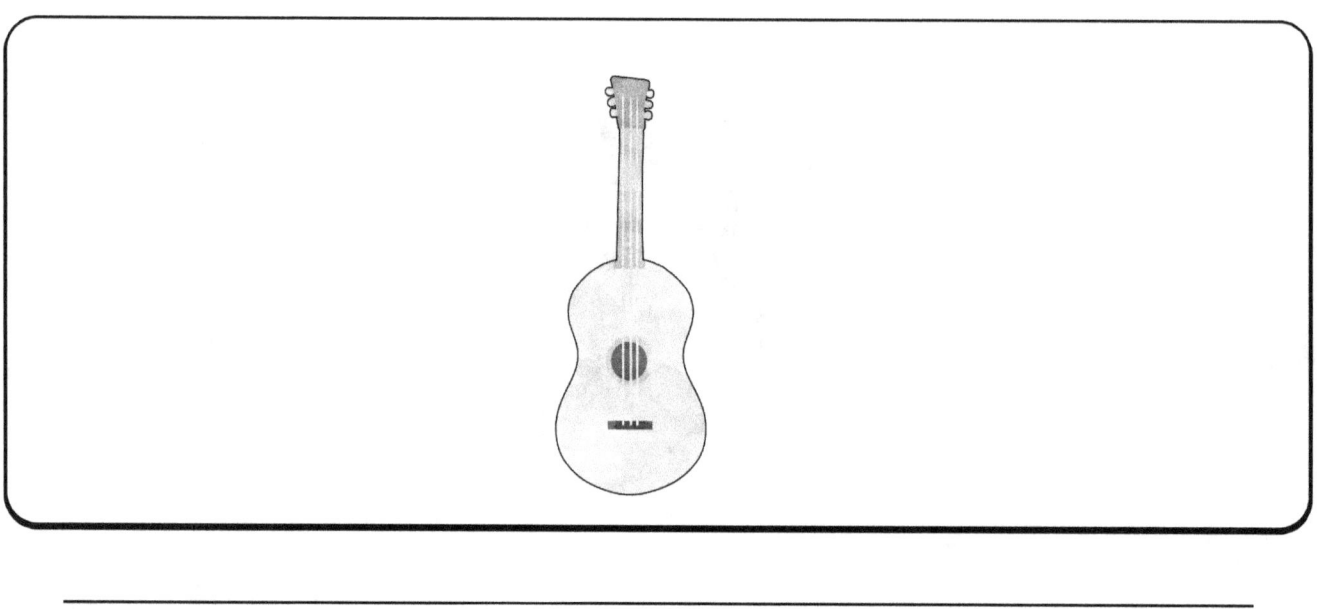

WRITE A SHORT STORY ABOUT WHAT YOU SEE

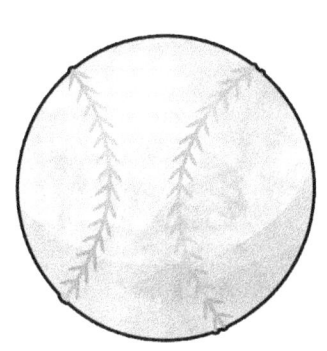

WRITE A SHORT STORY ABOUT WHAT YOU SEE

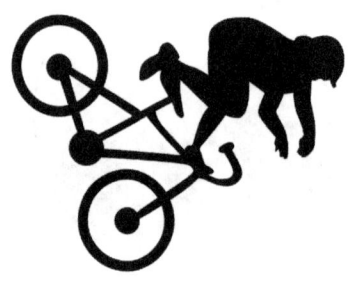

WRITE A SHORT STORY ABOUT WHAT YOU SEE

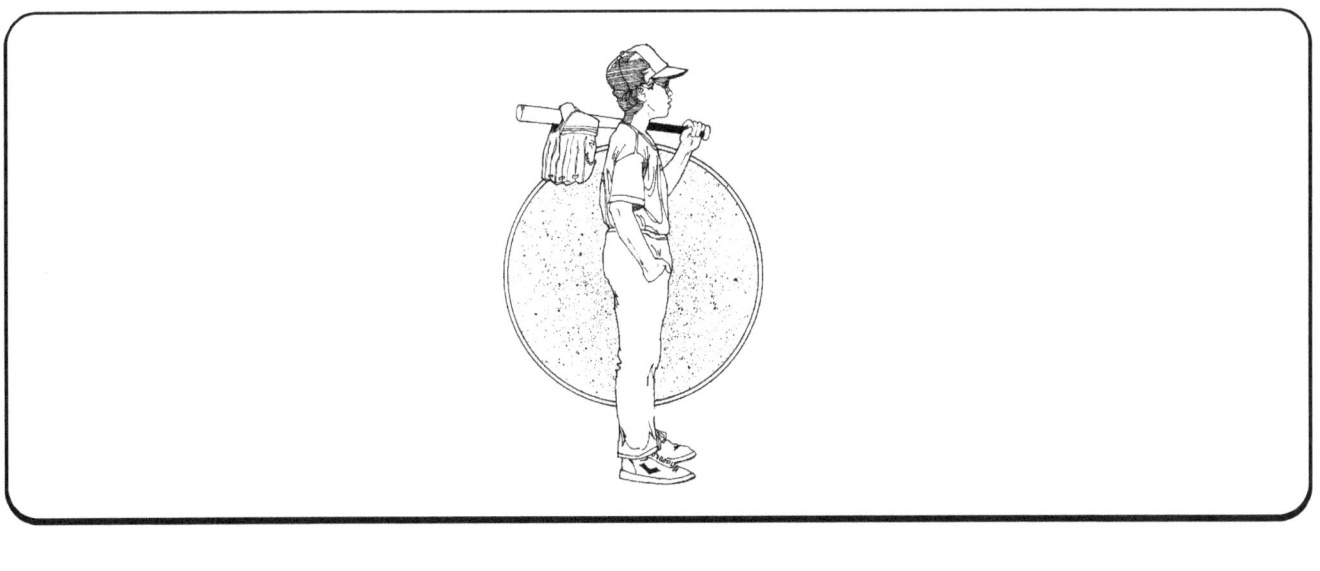

WRITE A SHORT STORY ABOUT WHAT YOU SEE

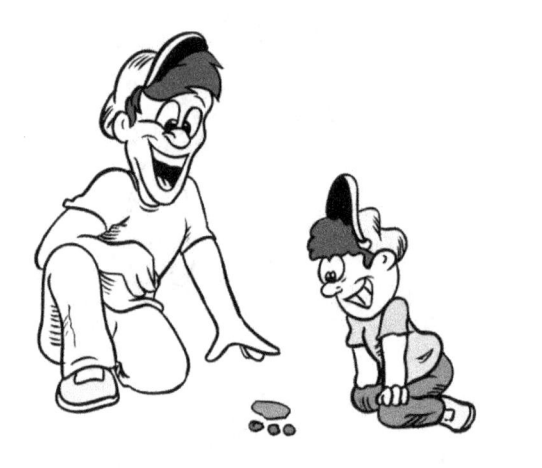

WRITE A SHORT STORY ABOUT WHAT YOU SEE

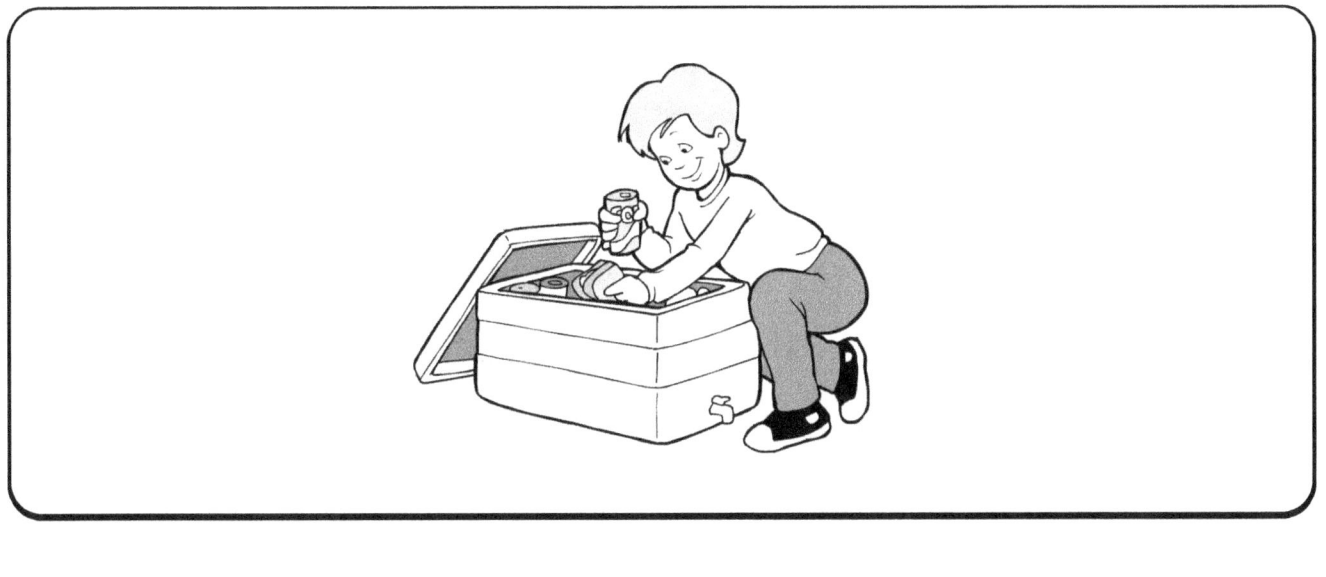

WRITE A SHORT STORY ABOUT WHAT YOU SEE

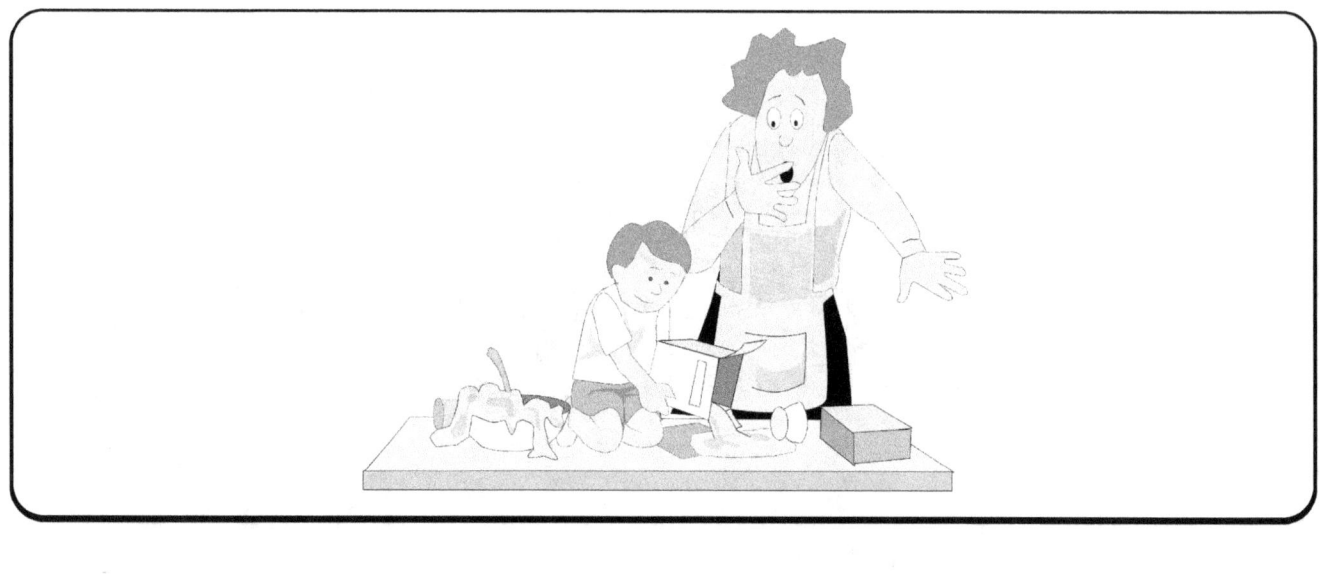

WRITE A SHORT STORY ABOUT WHAT YOU SEE

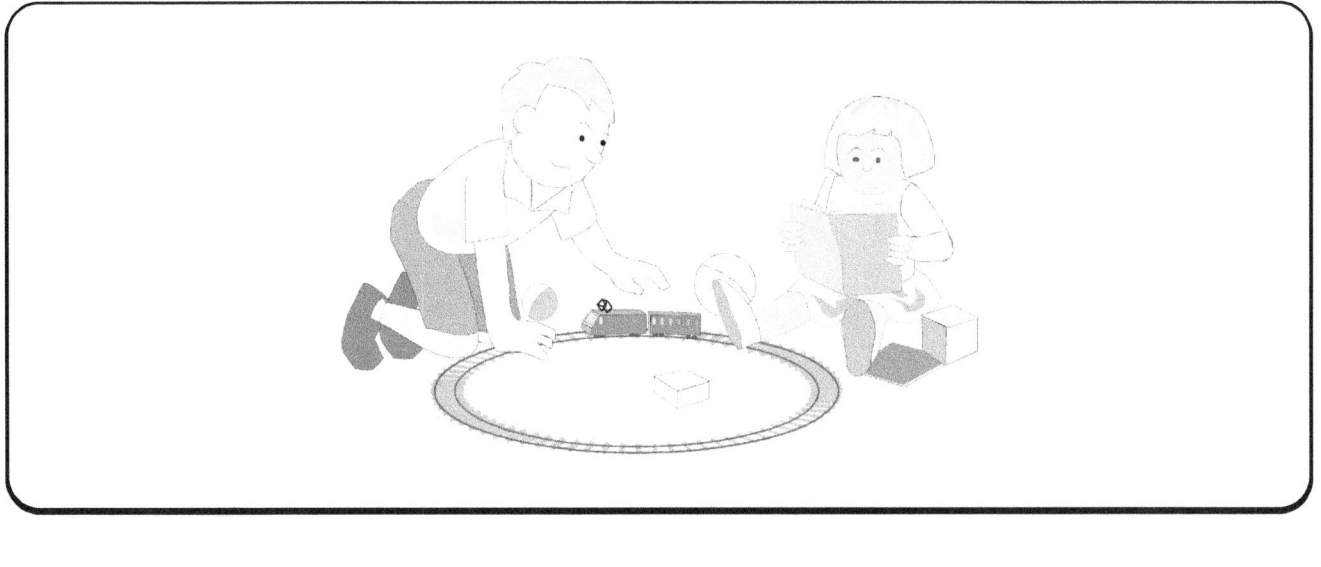

WRITE A SHORT STORY ABOUT WHAT YOU SEE

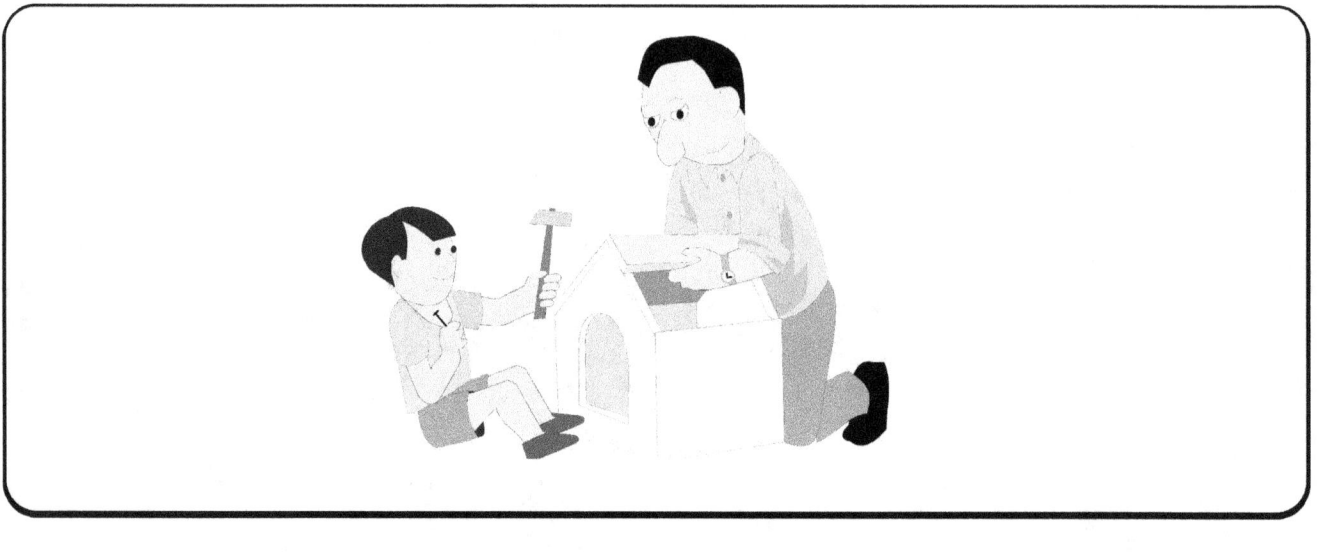

WRITE A SHORT STORY ABOUT WHAT YOU SEE

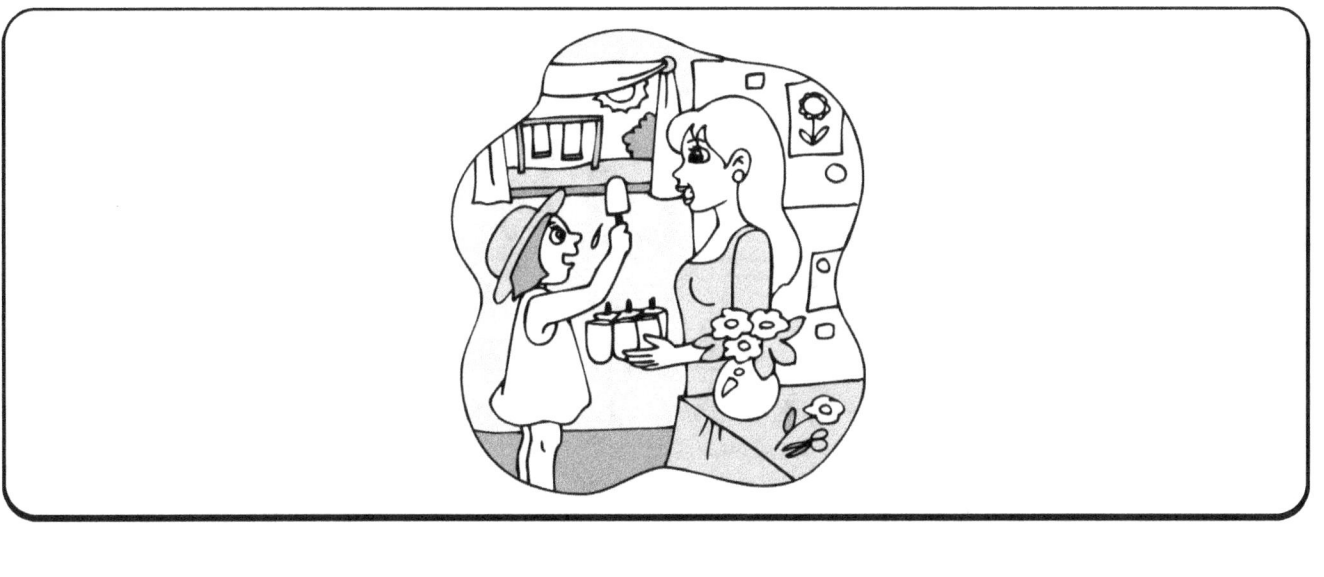

WRITE A SHORT STORY ABOUT WHAT YOU SEE

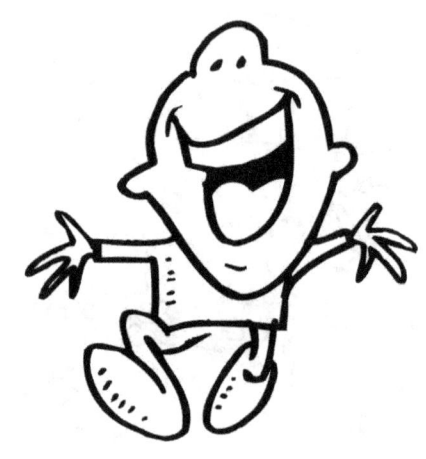

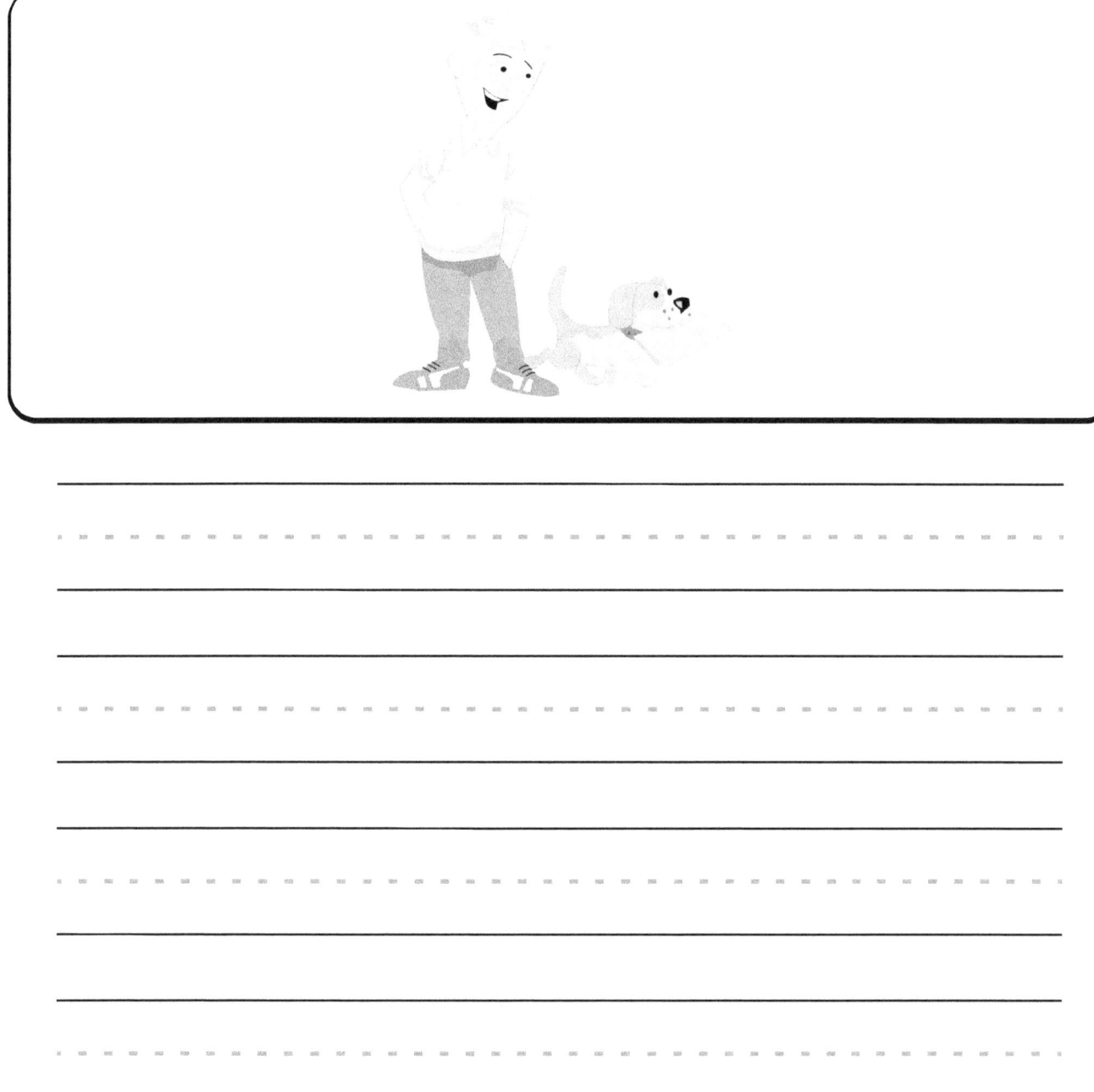

WRITE A SHORT STORY ABOUT WHAT YOU SEE

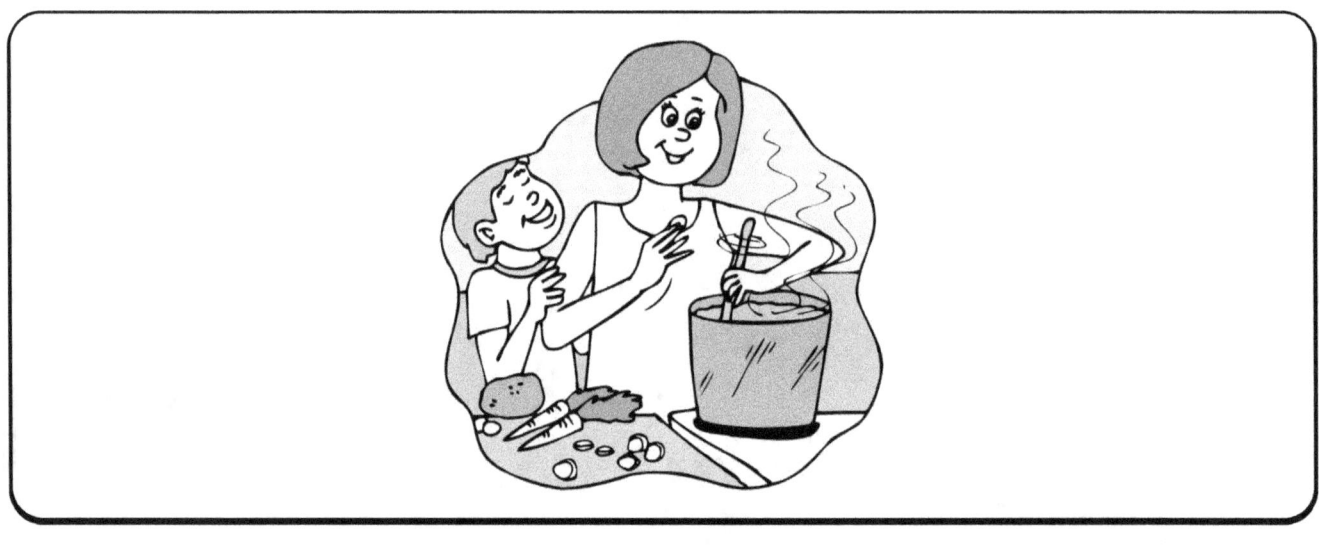

WRITE A SHORT STORY ABOUT WHAT YOU SEE

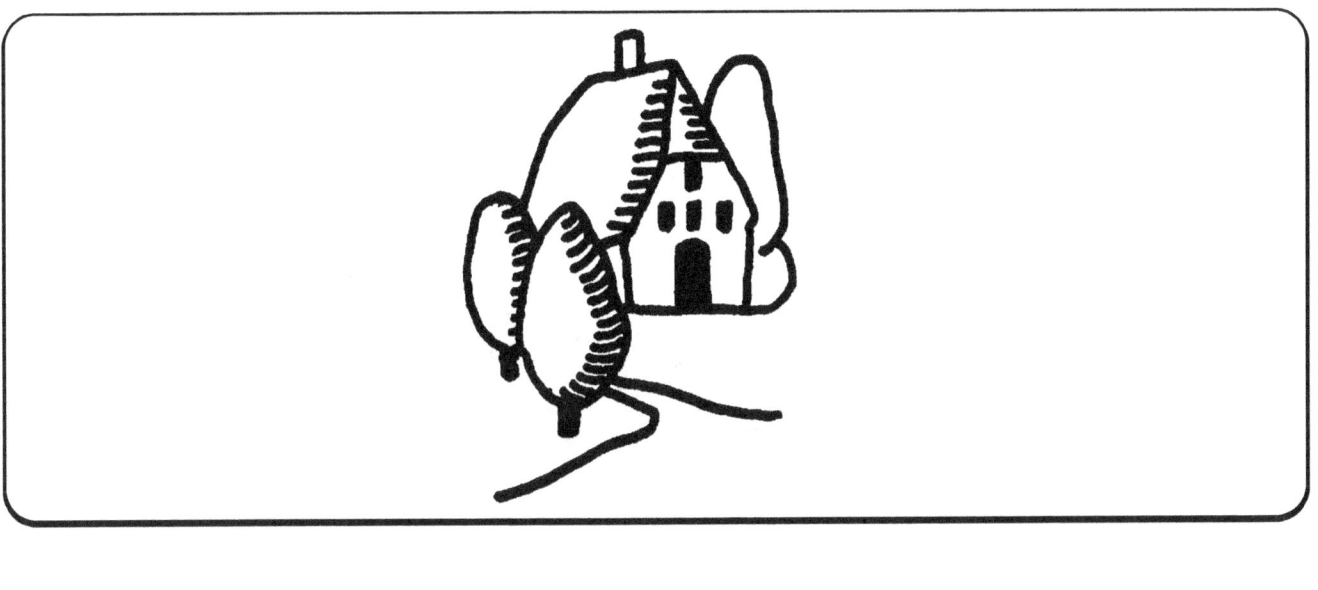

WRITE A SHORT STORY ABOUT WHAT YOU SEE

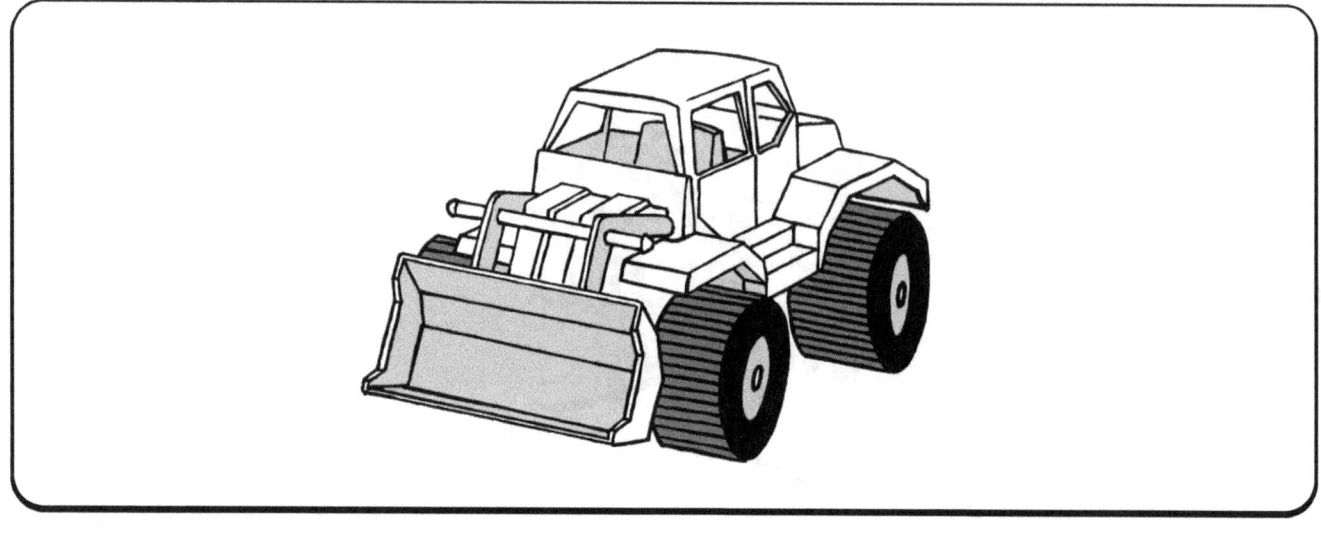

WRITE A SHORT STORY ABOUT WHAT YOU SEE

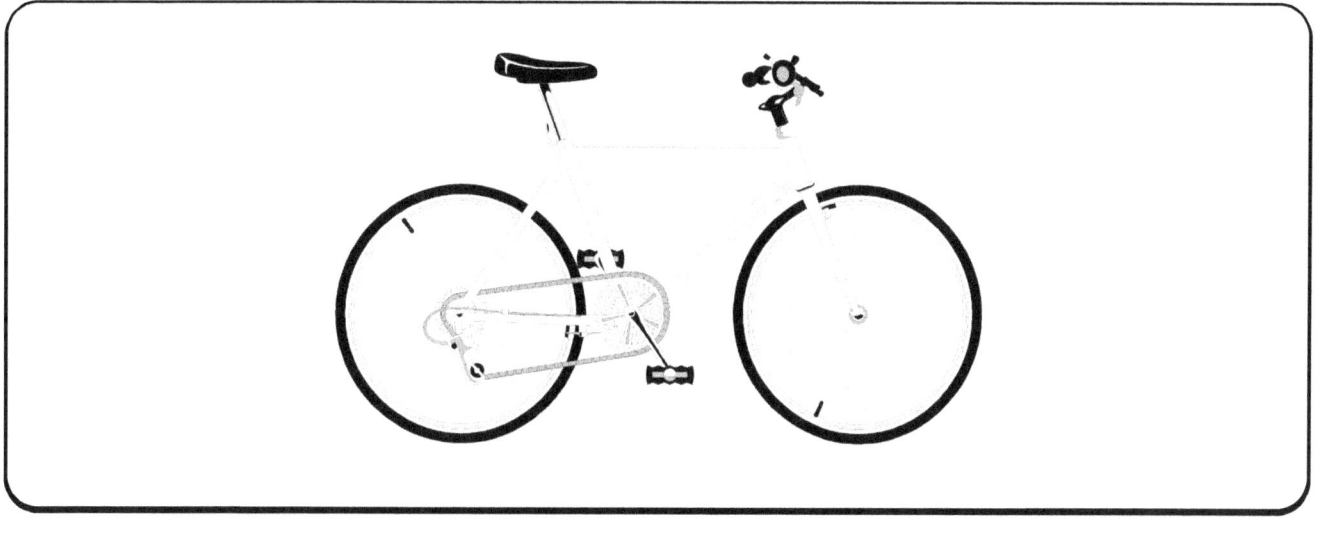

WRITE A SHORT STORY ABOUT WHAT YOU SEE

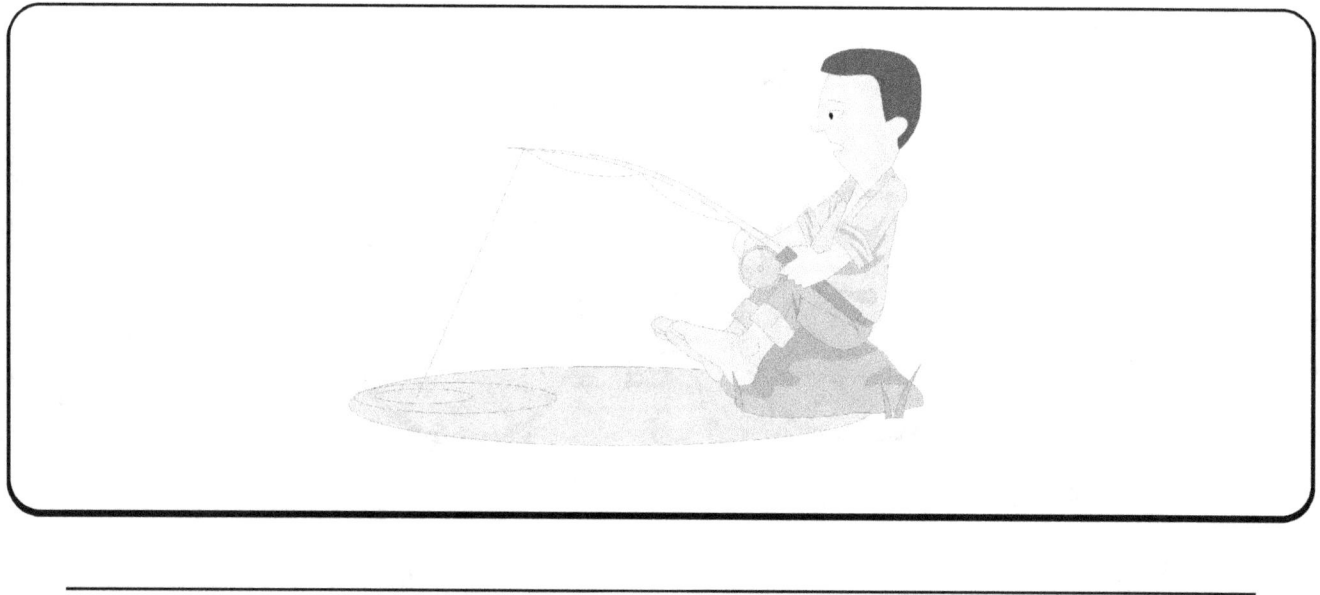

WRITE A SHORT STORY ABOUT WHAT YOU SEE

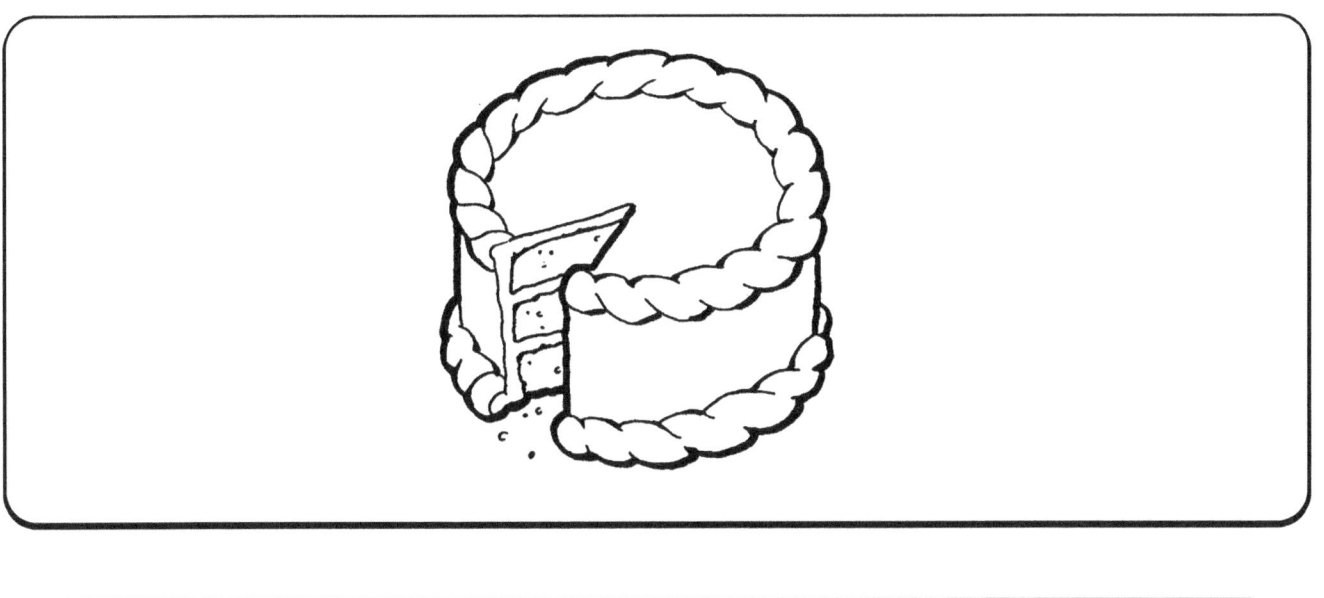

WRITE A SHORT STORY ABOUT WHAT YOU SEE

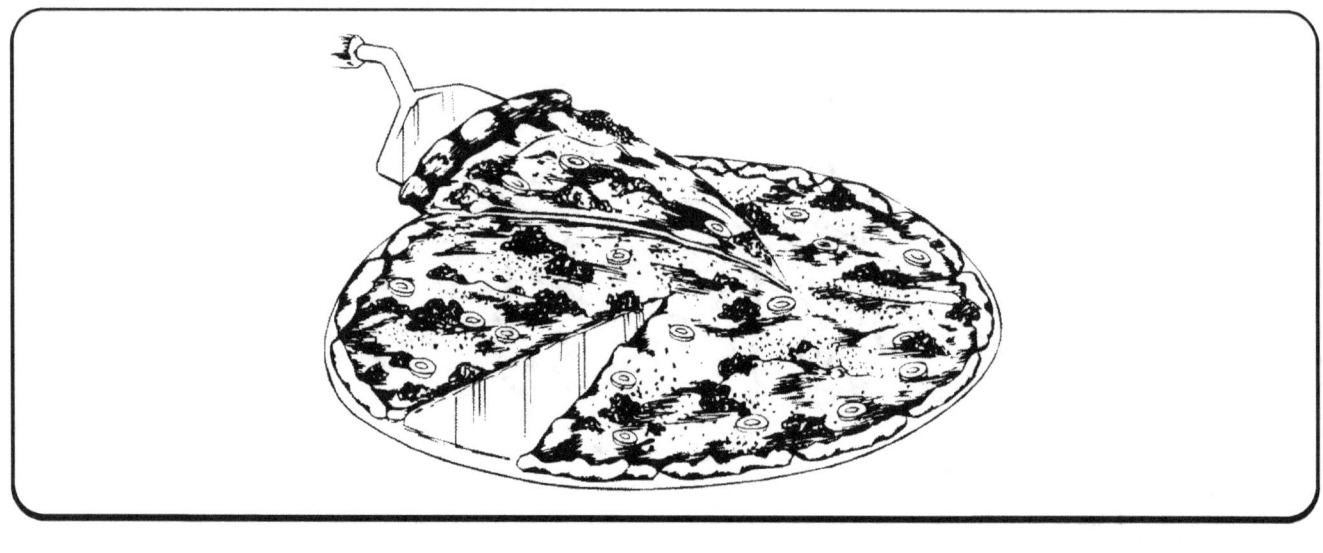

- -

- -

- -

- -

- -

WRITE A SHORT STORY ABOUT WHAT YOU SEE

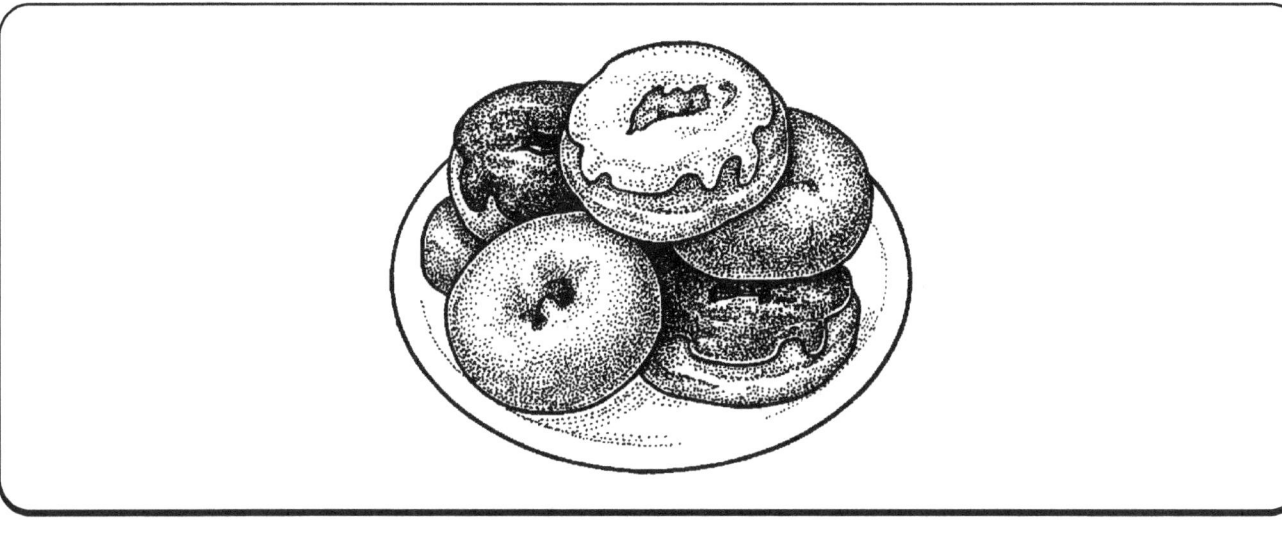

WRITE A SHORT STORY ABOUT WHAT YOU SEE

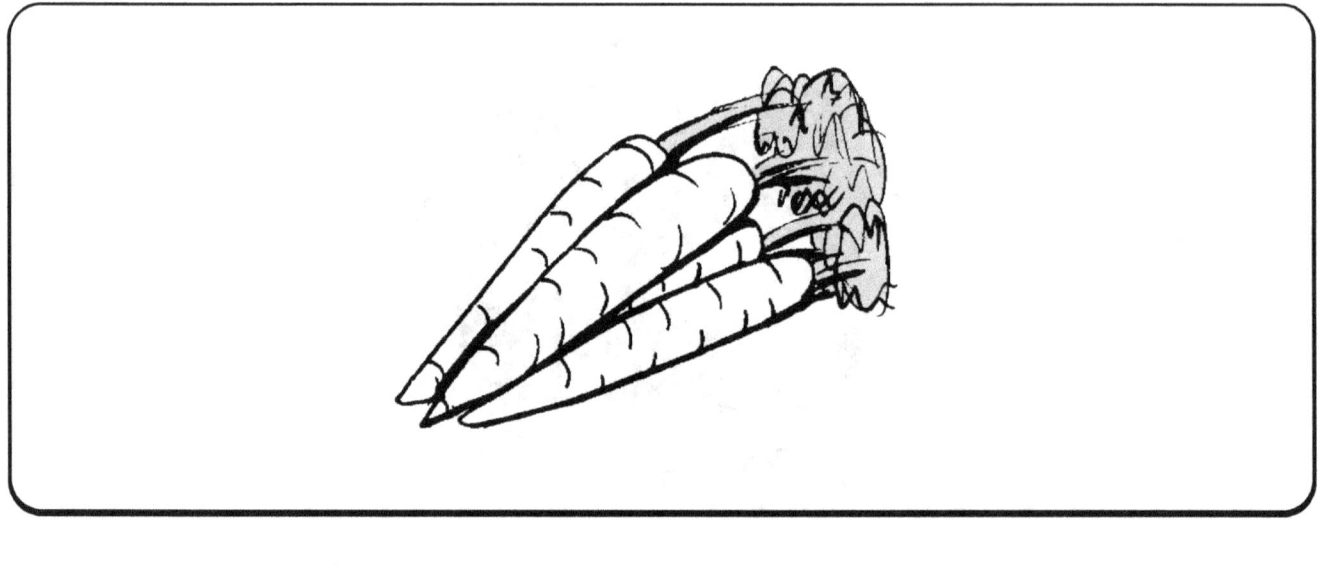

WRITE A SHORT STORY ABOUT WHAT YOU SEE

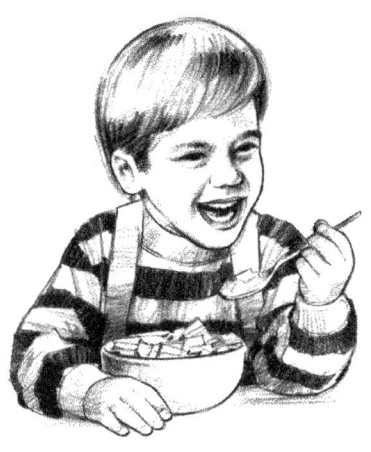

WRITE A SHORT STORY ABOUT WHAT YOU SEE

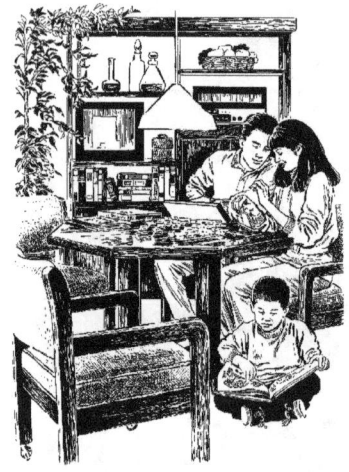

WRITE A SHORT STORY ABOUT WHAT YOU SEE

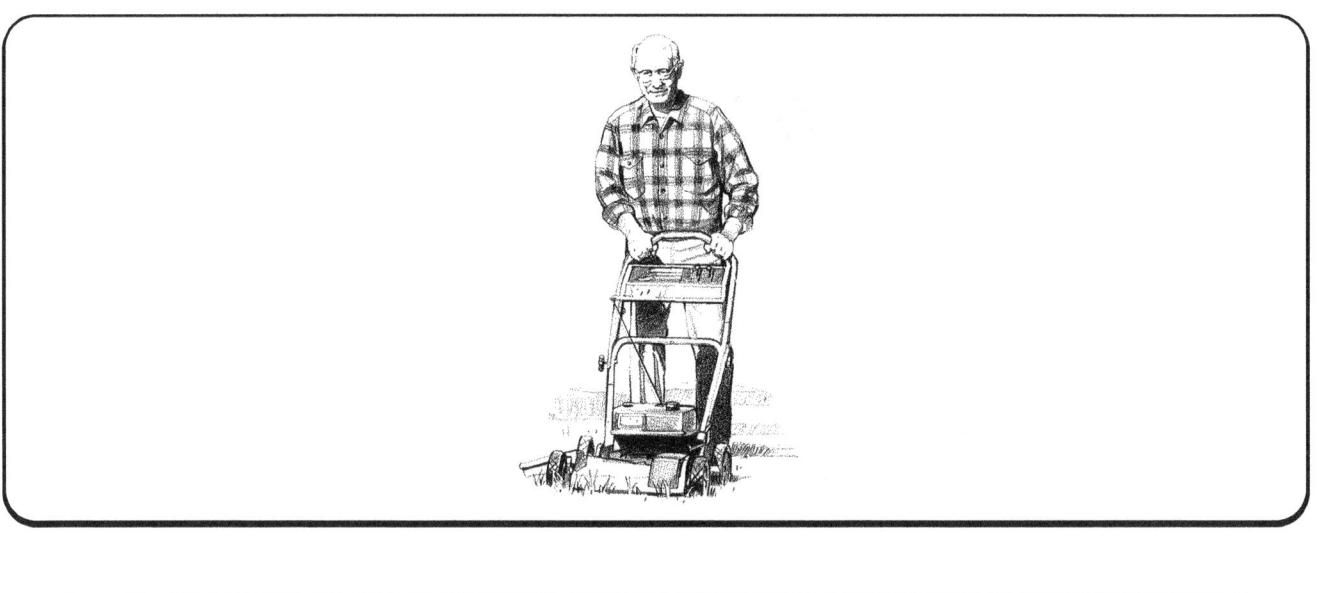

WRITE A SHORT STORY ABOUT WHAT YOU SEE

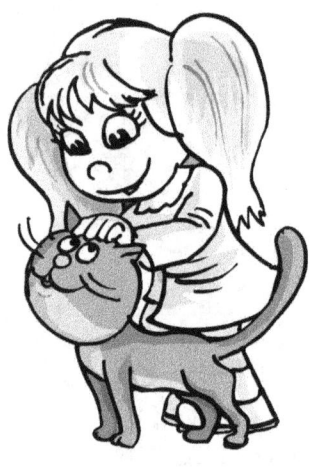

WRITE A SHORT STORY ABOUT WHAT YOU SEE

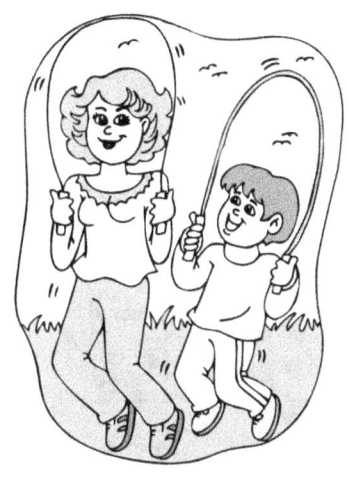

WRITE A SHORT STORY ABOUT WHAT YOU SEE

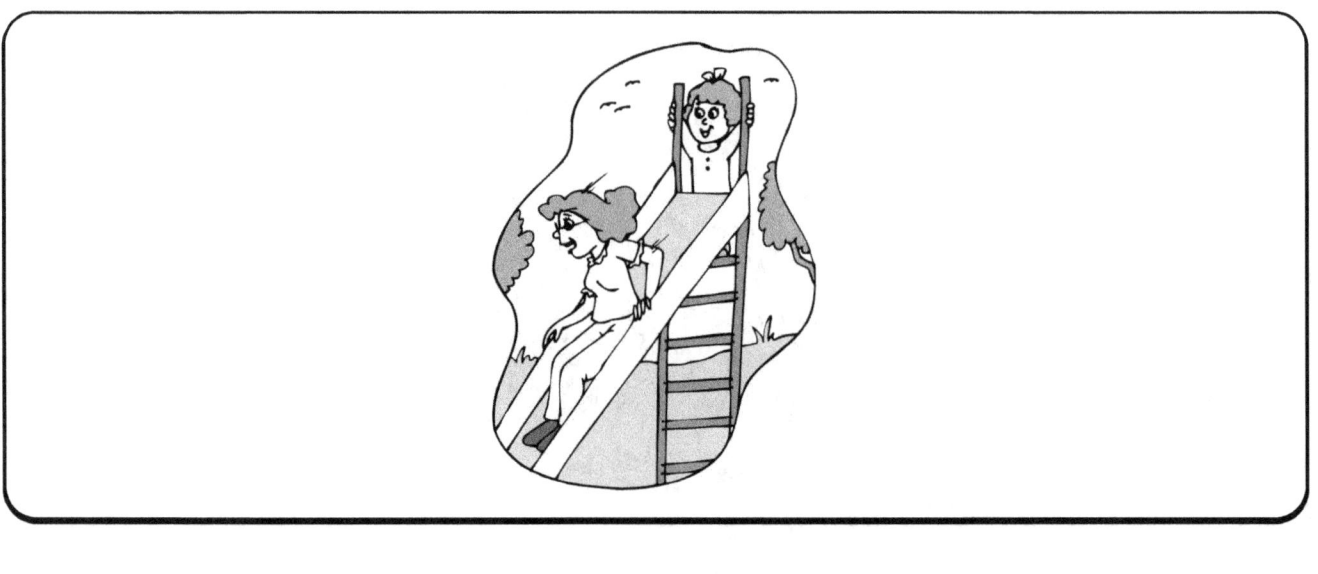

WRITE A SHORT STORY ABOUT WHAT YOU SEE

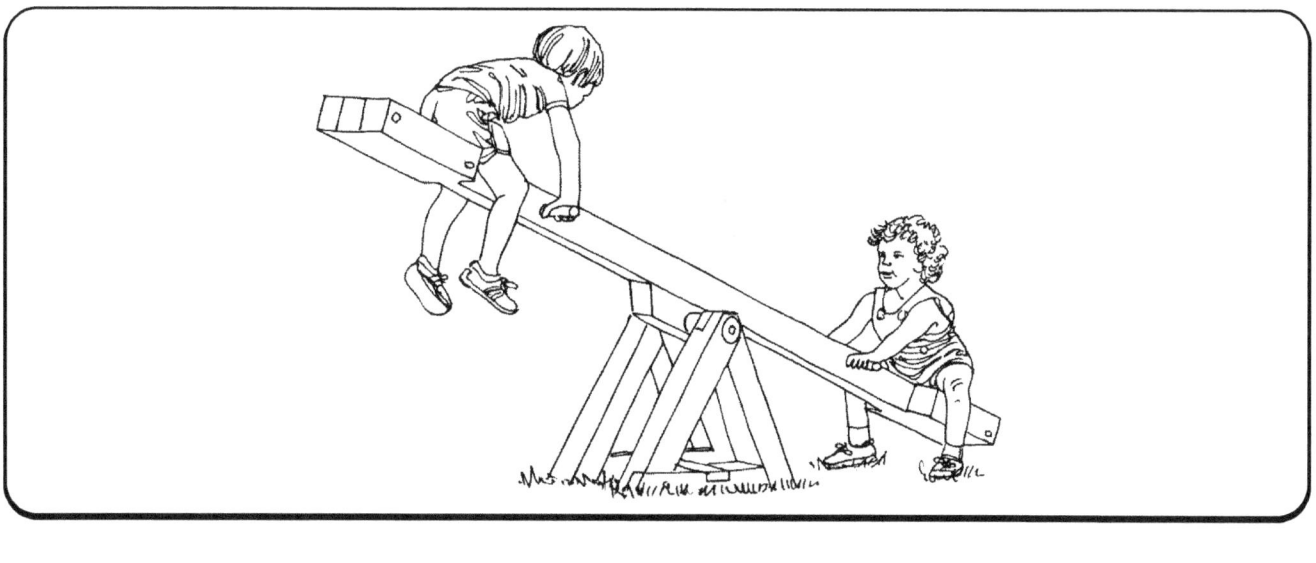

WRITE A SHORT STORY ABOUT WHAT YOU SEE

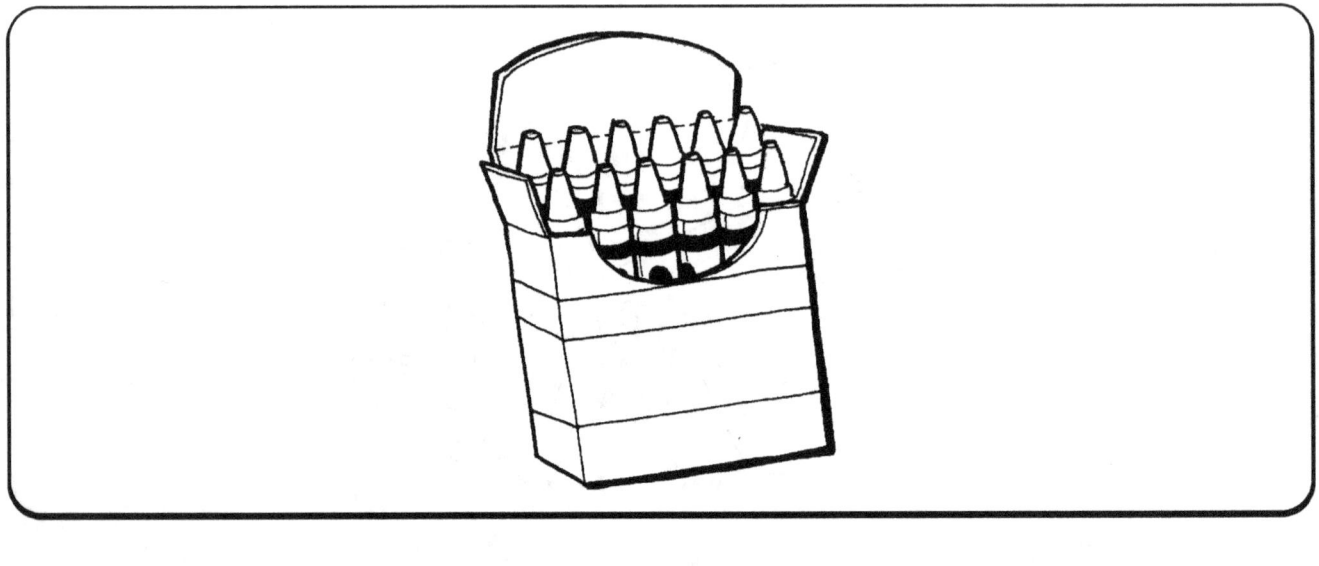

WRITE A SHORT STORY ABOUT WHAT YOU SEE

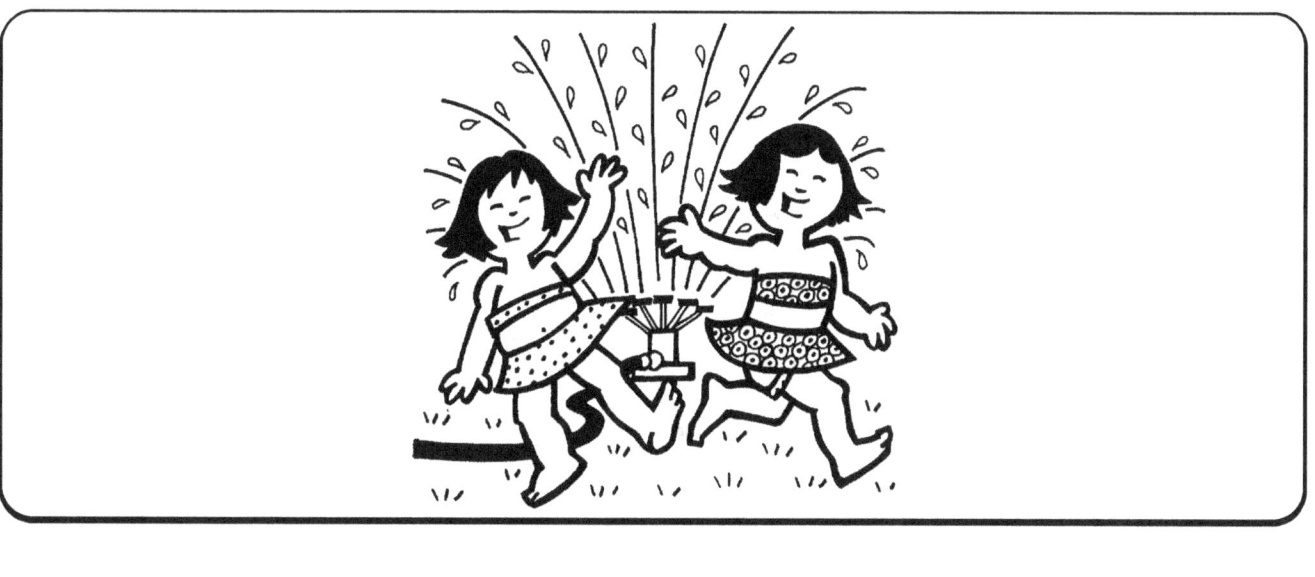

WRITE A SHORT STORY ABOUT WHAT YOU SEE

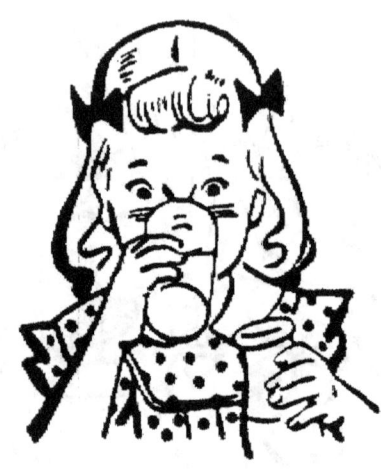

WRITE A SHORT STORY ABOUT WHAT YOU SEE

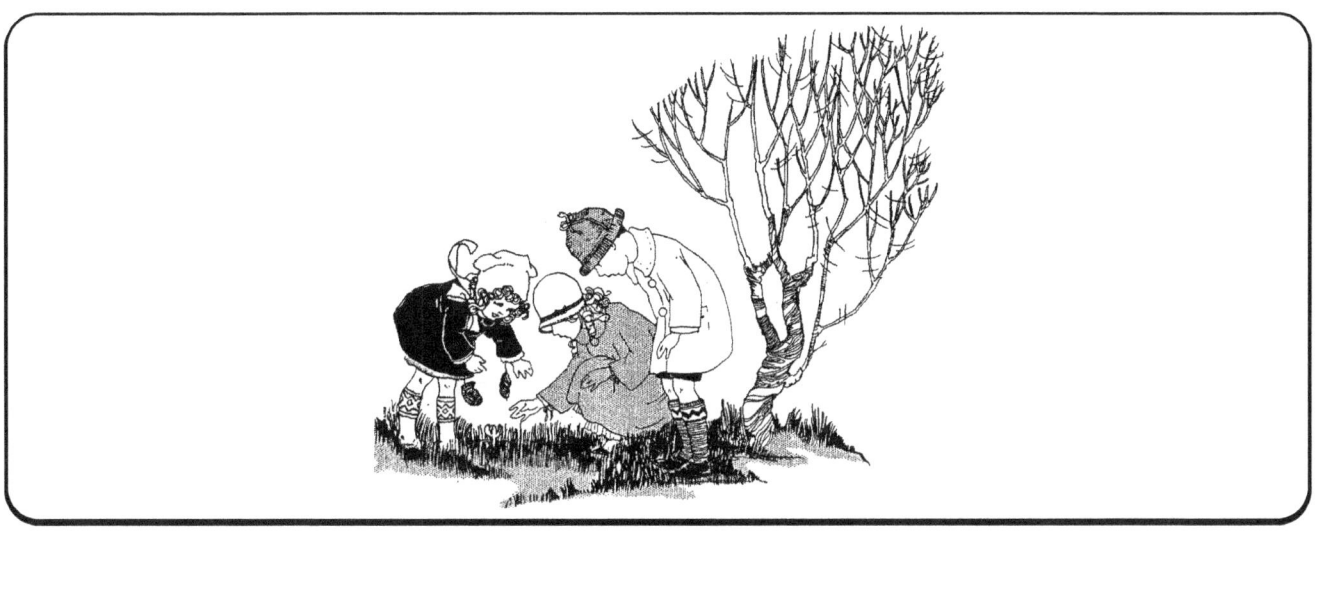

WRITE A SHORT STORY ABOUT WHAT YOU SEE

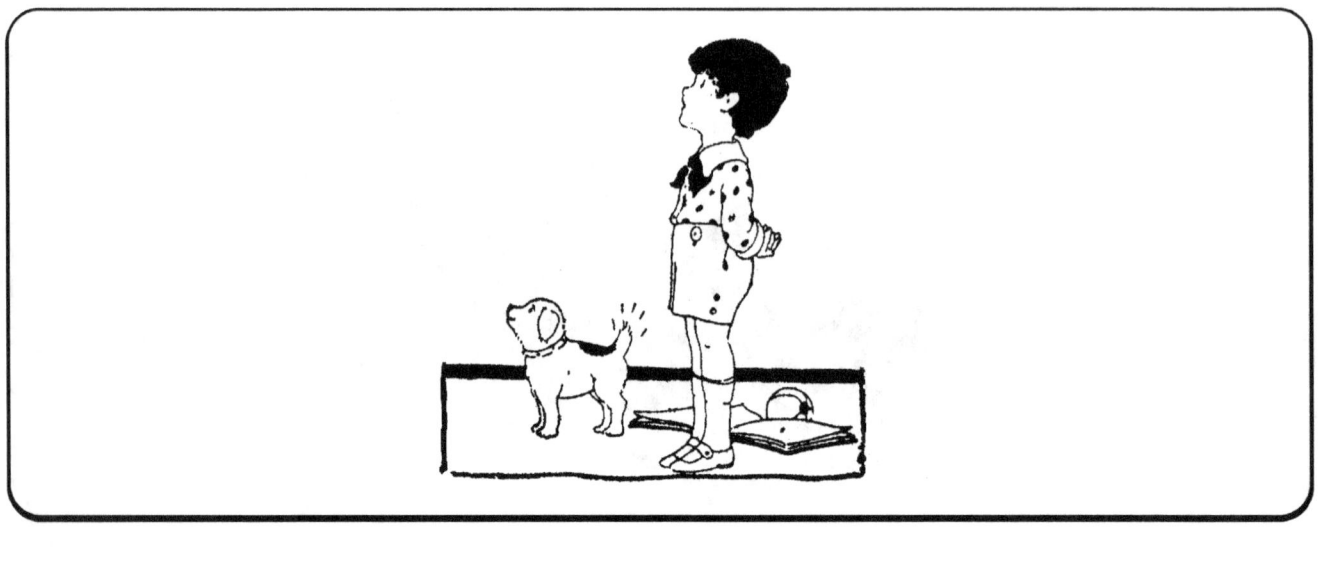

WRITE A SHORT STORY ABOUT WHAT YOU SEE

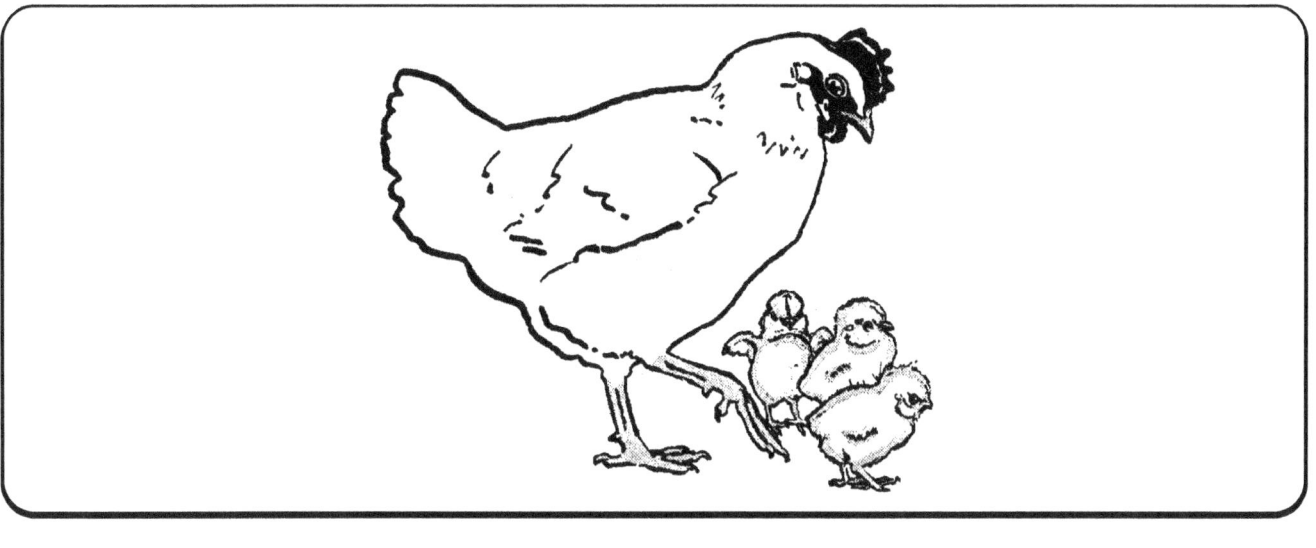